# What Are You Thinking?

## DR. MARK AGAN

ISBN-13: 978-1478281764
**Printed in the United States of America**

# CONTENTS

# INTRODUCTION

Johann von Goethe said, "To act is easy; to think is hard." Henry Ford said, "Thinking is the hardest work there is, which is probably the reason so few engage in it."

The reason your thoughts are important is because you become what captivates your mind. What you dwell upon will ultimately determine what you do.

Sometimes you will find that your mind is engaged in a battle, struggling to process feelings of anger, hurt, bitterness, or a host of other emotions you are experiencing.

At other times you will become a target of Satan by simply allowing your mind to become idle. As the old saying goes, "An idle mind is the Devil's playground."

So if that is the case, what can you do to keep your mind from becoming idle? And what can you do to protect yourself from the mental attacks you will face from Satan?

In this book we are going to look at what the mind is, how Satan attacks it, and specific things the Bible says you can do to win the battle of your mind.

# CHAPTER 1

# If I Only Had A Brain

Who can forget the famous song, *"If I Only Had A Brain,"* sung by the Scarecrow in *The Wizard of Oz?* I love the part that says, "…and my head I'd be scratchin' while my thoughts were busy hatchin' if I only had a brain."

Maybe you know someone that, when you look at them, you are tempted to say, "If they only had a brain!" You are not quite sure if they ever have any thoughts that, as the Scarecrow would say, are "busy hatchin'" up there. Some people may have a lot of knowledge in a particular area, but they don't seem to have a lot of common sense. Well, I guess we all have days where it seems like we have a difficult time getting our brains in gear.

## Brain Power

Every animal you can think of—mammals, birds, reptiles, fish, amphibians—has a brain. But the human brain is unique. It gives us the power to speak, imagine, and solve problems. It is truly an amazing thing. The brain can perform an incredible number of tasks. It controls body temperature, blood pressure, heart rate and breathing. It receives an abundance of information about the world around you from your various senses (seeing, hearing, smelling, tasting and touching). It handles your physical movement when walking, talking, standing or sitting. It lets you think, reason, dream, and experience emotions.

But there is a difference between your brain and your mind. In this book, my goal is to take a closer look at our mind and the battle we face with our thought life.

## Do You Mind?

So what exactly is the mind? Think of it this way: a computer requires hardware to perform its function. And the hardware needs software to make it run. Without software, hardware would be useless and without hardware, the software could not be used. The brain is like the hardware and the mind is like the software.

We sometimes use the words "brain" and "mind" interchangeably even though they really do refer to separate, although often overlapping, concepts. The brain is an organ but the mind isn't.

The brain is the physical place where the mind resides. The brain helps control your body but you use the mind to think.

The mind is where the manifestations of thought, perception, emotion, determination, memory, and imagination takes place within the brain. Because of this, it is where Satan wants most to get a foothold. If he can control your mind, he can control your actions. If he can control what you THINK, he can control what you DO. That is why the Bible says that our minds are to be renewed on a daily basis.

*And be not conformed to this world: but be ye transformed by the renewing of your mind, that ye may prove what is that good, and acceptable, and perfect, will of God. (Rom. 12:2)*

*And be renewed in the spirit of your mind; (Eph. 4:23)*

*For which cause we faint not; but though our outward man perish, yet the inward man is renewed day by day. (2 Cor. 4:16)*

Why is it important that our minds be renewed? Because when Adam and Eve fell in the garden and sin entered the world, man's mind was altered. The mind that was originally created to be guided by the Spirit, now follows after the flesh. And the more our minds follow after the flesh, the more it kills our lives spiritually.

Paul said, *"For they that are after the flesh do **mind** the things of the flesh; but they that are after the Spirit the things of the Spirit. For to be carnally **minded** is death; but to be spiritually **minded** is life and peace. Because the carnal **mind** is enmity against God: for it is not subject to the law of God, neither indeed can be"* (Rom. 8:5-7). The flesh has never wanted to obey God's laws and it never will.

If you allow your sinful mind to be guided by the flesh, it will always lead you away from God. You will never please God while following after the flesh. In fact, Paul goes on to say in the very next verse, *"So then they that are in the flesh cannot please God"* (Rom. 8:8). He doesn't say you can please Him only a little if you are in the flesh. He says the flesh *"cannot please God."*

## Put On Your Thinking Cap

As a child, I remember sitting there in that classroom while the teacher was teaching and before long my mind would begin to drift. It was especially bad if I was sitting near a window. My mind would easily wander away from school work to some childhood fantasy that featured me as the hero of the day saving some fair maiden in distress.

How could my teacher possibly expect me to focus on school when there was an imaginary adventure awaiting me? After all, everyone knows that maidens are more important than math. How many times would Lois Lane have been saved if Superman had been busy studying for a spelling bee?

I'm sure my teacher could sense this mental run-a-way train we were on because she would say to the class, "Ok, everyone put on your thinking caps." What she meant was, "Put your minds in gear. Get them ready to be used." The only problem was that my thinking cap never seemed to fit!

It is important that we put on our spiritual "thinking caps" because our thought life can make or break us, spiritually. The Bible says that a man is what he thinks in his heart (Prov. 23:7).

That is especially scary when you realize the Bible also teaches that *"The heart is deceitful above all things, and desperately wicked: who can know it?"* (Jer. 17:9).

The word *"heart"* also refers to our will and our intellect which would also include the mind. When sin came into this world, it came into our hearts and therefore into our minds. Because of sin, we now have the capacity to have our minds filled with anger, bitterness, lust, greed, jealousy, and a host of other sinful thoughts. Of course, let's not forget Satan's favorite pet sin, the sin of pride. Because of pride, we tend to think of ourselves more highly than we ought. As the saying goes, "You are what you think—not what you think you are."

Our thought life is very important because the Bible says that our ultimate goal should be to develop the mind of Christ. Paul said, *"Let this mind be in you, which was also in Christ Jesus:"* (Phil. 2:5). We must think like Christ if we are going to act like Christ, and the best way to think like Him is to read His Word. The more His Word gets into us, the more we begin to think as He thinks. That is why the Bible tells us to meditate on His Word.

*Blessed is the man that walketh not in the counsel of the ungodly, nor standeth in the way of sinners, nor sitteth in the seat of the scornful. But his delight is in the law of the LORD; and in his law doth he meditate day and night. (Ps. 1:1-2)*

As my schoolteacher could tell you, a child may read something, but that doesn't mean he understands it. The mind is like a stomach. It is not how much you put into it that counts, but how much it digests.

Dwight Pentecost said this about the importance of our thoughts:

*"The greatest area of sin in the believer's life is not the area of actions but the area of thought. There is a whole classification of sins that we would have to call sins of the mind. What was the first sin of Lucifer? It was pride. What is that? A sin of the mind. What is lust? A sin of the mind. What is covetousness? A sin of the mind. Greed? A sin of the mind. Suspicion? A sin of the mind. Discouragement? A sin of the mind. We could go on and on. Those sins are more real to the child of God than such sins as adultery and murder and theft. That is a testimony to the fact that there is a warfare going on. Satan is attacking the mind."*

Have you ever thought about the fact that the biggest battle we face is fought between our ears! Just think about the many veterans who have come back home after fighting in a war. Though they are safe at home, many fight a mental struggle that often results in nightmares and flashbacks that won't stop. What makes it so bad is the fact that they are no longer facing some foreign enemy in a jungle or desert, now the enemy is their own mind.

The mind can become an even tougher enemy than a physical person. With a physical enemy, there is the possibility that you can either defeat them or get away from them. But you cannot escape your own thoughts. Wherever you go your thoughts can go, too.

Since the mind is so powerful, it shouldn't surprise us that the Bible has much to say about it. For instance the Bible says:

**The ungodly mind is only evil.** Genesis 6:5 says, *"And GOD saw that the wickedness of man was great in the earth, and that every imagination of the thoughts of his heart was only evil continually."*

**Before salvation, we were enemies of God in our minds.** We didn't have to be taught to rebel. It was our nature to go against God.

*"And you, that were sometime alienated and enemies in your mind by wicked works, yet now hath he reconciled." (Col. 1:21)*

*"Among whom also we all had our conversation in times past in the lusts of our flesh, fulfilling the desires of the flesh and of the mind; and were by nature the children of wrath, even as others." (Eph. 2:3)*

**The mind can be a gate to deception and seduction.** Just like Eve, we must guard our mind from being deceived.

*"But I fear, lest by any means, as the serpent beguiled Eve through his subtilty, so your minds should be corrupted from the simplicity that is in Christ." (2 Cor. 11:3)*

**Do not let your mind be shaken or troubled about world events or the return of Christ.** Paul reminds us that God is still in control. Therefore, there is no need to fear what the future holds.

*"Now we beseech you, brethren, by the coming of our Lord Jesus Christ, and by our gathering together unto him, That ye be not soon shaken in mind, or be troubled, neither by spirit, nor by word, nor by letter as from us, as that the day of Christ is at hand." (2 Thess. 2:1-2)*

**We are to be of one mind with other believers.** The Bible says in 1 Peter 3:8, *"Finally, be ye all of one mind, having compassion one of another, love as brethren, be pitiful, be courteous:"*

**Our mind should be ready to receive God's Word.** Acts 17:11 says, *"These were more noble than those in Thessalonica, in that <u>they received</u> the word with all readiness of mind, and searched the scriptures daily, whether those things were so."*

**We are to love God with all of our mind.** Jesus said in Matthew 22:37, *"Thou shalt love the Lord thy God with all thy heart, and with all thy soul, and with all thy mind."*

## The First Step

Let me say that if you do not know Jesus Christ as your personal Savior, you will never have the power to control your thought life that you could have through Him. Right now, your mind is against the things of God. Paul reminded the believers at Colosse of this very fact. He said, *"And you, that were sometime alienated and enemies in your mind by wicked works, yet now hath he reconciled"* (Col. 1:21).

So the first step toward controlling your mind and your thought life is to put your faith and trust in Jesus

Christ as your Savior. Until then, you will never understand spiritual things. The Bible says that *"...the natural man receiveth not the things of the Spirit of God: for they are foolishness unto him: neither can he know them, because they are spiritually discerned"* (1 Cor. 2:14).

The great painter, Thomas Kinkade, was known as "the painter of light." He painted some of the most beautiful scenery one could think up. They were always scenes so serene and peaceful that it was easy to imagine yourself living there, or at least wanting to.

As much as I love Thomas Kinkade's paintings, I could not paint like him if you paid me a million dollars! Believe me. I wish I could! The trouble is, I do not *think* like he did. My mind does not process all of the steps needed to make that happen.

However, if doctors could somehow transplant his brain and thought process into my head and literally give me the mind of Thomas Kinkade, then I would be able to think like him and could easily accomplish what would be an otherwise impossible task.

The same is true spiritually. One cannot understand spiritual things until the Spirit of God is living inside him. Once you have the Spirit of God living inside you, then you will begin to *think* like God and will begin to have the mind of God.

Once we begin thinking like God, then we can know the will of God. The Bible says, *"that ye might be filled with the knowledge of his will in all wisdom and spiritual understanding;"* (Col. 1:9). The reason many do not know God's will for their lives is because they do not have the *"spiritual understanding"* that comes from the Holy Spirit.

"If I only had a brain." Well, you do have a brain and you also have a mind; a mind the Bible says needs to be **guided** and **guarded** against the attacks of Satan. In the next chapter we will take a closer look at the enemy who is attacking us mentally.

# CHAPTER 2

# The Invisible Enemy

It happened one Sunday night around 9:40 pm. When police arrived at the home, the family was already dead. Although crime scenes are a common thing to police, this one was different. In fact, you would have never guessed just by looking that anything was wrong.

The father was sitting in his chair in front of the television set and his two children were lying beside him. Everything seemed normal. The television was still on as were the lights from the recently decorated Christmas tree.

What baffled police was the fact that there seemed to be no evidence of foul play. There was no evidence of a break-in. No evidence of a struggle. Actually, there was no evidence at all! What had killed this father, his two children and even the family dogs?

It was later determined that they were killed by an invisible killer. One that is quiet, undetectable and completely lethal. They died from carbon monoxide poisoning. Carbon monoxide is a toxic gas, but being colorless, odorless, and tasteless, it is very difficult for people to detect.

In the spiritual realm, there is also an invisible enemy; one who cannot be seen with your eyes or felt with your hands, but is real just the same. This invisible enemy is Satan and he is attacking the minds of men, women, boys, and girls. He is constantly trying to tear apart our families and our churches.

So the bad news is that we have an enemy, but the good news is that we can have victory over our enemy.

*But thanks be to God, which giveth us the victory through our Lord Jesus Christ. (1 Cor. 15:57)*

Yes, we can have the victory, but in order to get the victory, we must know our enemy! A key component to the success of any sports team is knowing the opponent.

The more you know about how they play the game, the better prepared you will be to guard against their advances.

Likewise, we must know our *spiritual* opponent. We must learn how he operates, what his strategies are, and how to defend ourselves against the weapons he will use against us.

The Bible says we should be on our guard *"Lest Satan should get an advantage of us: for we are not ignorant of his devices"* (2 Cor. 2:11). More times than not, when people fall into sin it is because they let their guard down; they were *"ignorant of his devices."*

Why is this so important? Because, unlike in sports, this is no game. This is serious business. It is life or death!

## Satan Is Real

The biblical teaching about the reality of Satan is being watered down in many churches, today. Many are trying to say that Satan is not real because if they can convince themselves that Satan doesn't exist, then Hell does not exist either.

But just as surely as the Bible teaches there is a literal Satan, it also teaches there is a literal place called Hell.

*I am he that liveth, and was dead; and, behold, I am
alive for evermore, Amen; and have the keys of hell
and of death. (Rev. 1:18)*

When speaking of the judgment that is to come, the
Bible says, *"And the sea gave up the dead which were in it;
and death and hell delivered up the dead which were in
them: and they were judged every man according to their
works. And death and hell were cast into the lake of fire.
This is the second death"* (Rev. 20:13-14).

If you accept the Scriptures as the divinely inspired
Word of God rather than merely a record of man's
thoughts about God, then you cannot deny the reality of
Satan. Seven books of the Old Testament teach of his
reality: Genesis, 1 Chronicles, Job, Psalms, Isaiah,
Ezekiel, and Zechariah. Every writer of the New
Testament affirmed his reality. Christ's teaching also
assumes and affirms Satan's existence.

To show that he is a real person, he is given
distinctive traits of personality, including intellect (2 Cor.
11:3; Luke 4:1f.). Ascribed to him are the emotions of:
desire (Luke 22:31; cf. Isa. 14:12f.), jealousy (Job 1:8, 9),
hatred (1 Peter 4:8), anger (Rev. 12:12), and will. The
Devil commands (Luke 4:3, 9) and leads rebellions (Rev.
12:1-3).

## Where Did He Come From?

The Scriptures teach that, before man and the world were created, God had created an *"innumerable company of angels"* (Hebrews 12:22). The highest of these spiritual beings are the cherubim, who are attendants at the very throne of God, and the *"anointed cherub"* at that throne was Lucifer himself (Ezekiel 28:14).

Satan was originally created as an angel named Lucifer. The word "angel" means "messenger." All angels were created by God. The Bible says, *"For by him were all things created, that are in heaven, and that are in earth, visible and invisible, whether they be thrones, or dominions, or principalities, or powers: all things were created by him, and for him:"* (Col.1:16).

Though God did create all angels, He did not create Lucifer as an evil being. The angels, like man, were created as free spirits, not as mechanical robots. They had the capability to reject God's will and rebel against His authority if they should choose to do so. Lucifer chose to do so. Not only did *he* choose to rebel, he also led a third of all the other angels in a rebellion as well.

Lucifer was perfect until he sinned. Ezekiel 28:15 says, *"Thou wast perfect in thy ways from the day that thou wast created, till iniquity was found in thee."* So where did sin begin? It began in Lucifer's heart.

*"Thine heart was lifted up because of thy beauty, thou hast corrupted thy wisdom by reason of thy brightness: I will cast thee to the ground, I will lay thee before kings, that they may behold thee" (Ezek. 28:17).*

As a result of Satan's rebellion, he was cast out of Heaven. God still rules over the world, but within limitations, He allows Lucifer, now called Satan, to exercise power over it.

*And the devil said unto him, All this power will I give thee, and the glory of them: for that is delivered unto me; and to whomsoever I will I give it. (Luke 4:6)*

*Now is the judgment of this world: now shall the prince of this world be cast out. (John 12:31)*

*In whom the god of this world hath blinded the minds of them which believe not, lest the light of the glorious gospel of Christ, who is the image of God, should shine unto them. (2 Cor. 4:4)*

*Wherein in time past ye walked according to the course of this world, according to the prince of the power of the air, the spirit that now worketh in the children of disobedience: (Eph. 2:2)*

## What Is He Doing Now?

Ever since he lost his position in Heaven, he has been actively trying to thwart God's plan of redemption. His first goal is to keep people from hearing about Jesus Christ and His death, burial, and resurrection. If he cannot keep someone from trusting in Jesus Christ as their Savior, then he does the next best thing. He seeks to ruin their lives by leading them into sin so that their testimony will be ineffective toward leading others to Christ.

I remember as a child seeing that famous Army recruitment poster that had a picture of Uncle Sam on the front pointing his finger at me saying, "I Want YOU!" Then in smaller letters underneath it read, "For the U.S. Army." When I think of Satan, I think of that poster. That is what Satan is saying to us, "I want YOU." He is after us and he wants to destroy us. That is why the Bible warns us to *"Be sober, be vigilant; because your adversary the devil, as a roaring lion, walketh about, seeking whom he may devour:"* (1 Pet. 5:8).

The most notable instance of Satan's intentions is found in Job 1:6-7, *"Now there was a day when the sons of God came to present themselves before the LORD, and Satan came also among them. And the LORD said unto Satan, Whence comest thou? Then Satan answered the*

*LORD, and said, From going to and fro in the earth, and from walking up and down in it."*

He evidently has free rein to roam the earth looking for someone he can trouble. He is constantly on the lookout for those who will give in to his wicked ways or be sympathetic toward his evil deeds.

The first resort of a deceitful heart is to find someone else that is just as deceitful. Since Satan found it easy to rebel against God, he goes about searching for others who might have the same seeds of rebellion germinating just below the surface.

Charles Spurgeon, in his book *Power Over Satan*, said, "When Satan looks at the Christian and finds him faithful to God and to His truth…He seems to say, 'I, a prince, a peer of God's parliament, would not submit my will to the Almighty. I thought it better to reign in hell than serve in heaven. I did not keep my proper domain, but fell from my throne. How is it that these stand? What grace is it that keeps these? I was a vessel of gold, and yet I was broken. These are earthen vessels, but I cannot break them!'"

Since he does not always find a willing partner in his wickedness, he must rely on his cunning, sly manner to dupe the unsuspecting.

20

## He Is A Sneaky Enemy

The longer you do something the better you get at doing it. Well, the reason Satan is so good at deceiving us is because he has been at this for a long time. God knows how dangerous Satan can be. That's why the Bible says, *"Put on the whole armour of God, that ye may be able to stand against the wiles of the devil"* (Eph. 6:11). We would not need the *"armour of God"* if Satan were not dangerous.

So what exactly are we supposed to be watching out for? We are to be watching out for *"the wiles of the devil."* The word *"wiles"* is referring to Satan's methods or tactics. Here's what that means: Satan does not just go around willy-nilly trying to trick you hoping that it works. He does not come to you face-to-face. He advances covertly; he likes to work under the cover of darkness so his deeds cannot be easily detected.

Satan is no dummy. He has a systematic way to go about seducing your children. He has strategically planned how he is going to tear up your home. He has a plan on how to destroy your marriage. "Well, don't you worry, preacher, I can handle it." No you can't! Don't be deceived!

The Bible says we are not to be ignorant of Satan's devices. The way we prepare to fight an armed man is totally different than the way we would prepare to fight a deadly virus. You cannot fight a virus with bullets. As soon as you think you are safe, that is when you are most vulnerable. Paul warns us in 1 Corinthians 10:12, *"Wherefore let him that thinketh he standeth take heed lest he fall."* If Satan could deceive one third of the angels who had never sinned and who dwelt in the very presence of God, then he can deceive you.

The very same pride that caused Satan's downfall will cause yours, too! The Bible says, *"Pride goeth before destruction, and an haughty spirit before a fall"* (Prov. 16:18). The word *"haughty"* means arrogant. When a person gets to the point where they feel they can handle Satan's attacks without God's help, they have an arrogant spirit. Once they have an arrogant spirit, it will not be long before they will fall.

## He Is A Strong Enemy

Satan is strong. He is not someone you can take on alone. Paul described how powerful a force we are up against when he wrote, *"For we wrestle not against flesh and blood, but against principalities, against powers, against the rulers of the darkness of this world..."* (Eph. 6:12).

The words *"Principalities"* and *"powers"* refers to leader's in Satan's army. He has those who are wholly devoted to him just as God has those who are wholly devoted to Him.

You and I do not have what it takes to defeat Satan alone. Satan has no mercy. He will show no mercy on your family, your marriage, your ministry, your church, or even your pastor. We cannot face Satan in our own strength. Make no mistake about it, Satan is powerful, but he is not ALL-POWERFUL!

That is why it is important that we are faithful to church. When we constantly miss the preaching of God's Word, we are in fact cutting off our supply of spiritual protection. See, the Word of God helps us understand our enemy and how Satan's attacks. So the more we learn the Word of God, the better prepared we are at facing his attacks. Why do you think Satan makes it so difficult for you to read your Bible? Because it blows his cover!

## He Is A Spiritual Enemy

Paul said that *"we wrestle not against flesh and blood, but against principalities, against powers, against the rulers of the darkness of this world, against* **spiritual wickedness** *in high places"* (Eph. 6:12).

Satan is spiritual and to make it worse, he is invisible! We are not fighting the rap music industry; we are fighting Satan! We are not fighting the movie industry; we are fighting Satan! We are not fighting the pornography industry; we are fighting Satan! Our REAL battle is with Satan, the *"prince of the power of the air"* (Eph. 2:2).

In fact, there is a spiritual warfare going on right here while you are reading. The very fact that you are reading this book shows that you have a desire to let Christ control your thought life. It is obviously your desire to draw closer to God. Well, any time you begin to make a move toward God, Satan is going to attack you and your efforts.

Satan is not after the drunk on the streets; he already has him! He is not after the drug addict who has sold his soul for another fix. He is after those who are trying to do something for God. We are fighting a spiritual battle because it is being fought by a spiritual enemy. That is why the Bible says, *"For the weapons of our warfare are not carnal, but mighty through God to the pulling down of strong holds;"* (2 Cor. 10:4).

Satan is at work behind the scenes to get a stronghold of sin built up in your life. Therefore, worldly weapons will not suffice. We must fight spiritual battles with spiritual weapons.

*Finally, my brethren, be strong in the Lord, and in the power of his might. (Eph. 6:10)*

Satan does not want you to know that you can be strong in the Lord. He does not want you to realize what a power source you have available to you. You see, it is not MY strength I am depending on, it is GOD's strength! If you are depending upon YOUR strength, you're in trouble.

How can we guard ourselves from pornography, lust, covetousness, adultery or fornication? By depending upon God's strength. How you will keep your marriage clean and pure? By depending upon God's strength.

While we are no match for Satan by ourselves, we know we can overcome his snares because the Bible says, *"Ye are of God, little children, and have overcome them: because greater is he that is in you, than he that is in the world"* (1 John 4:4).

The Apostle Paul also reminded us of the power we have in Christ when he wrote in Philippians 4:13, *"I can do all things through Christ which strengtheneth me."* The key is not that *"I can do all things"*; that is nothing more than humanistic philosophy by itself. They key is *"through Christ which strengtheneth me."* The strength we get to *"do all things"* does not come from us. It comes from the Lord.

From the experiences of Paul's life, he comes to the general conclusion that he could *"do all things through Christ."* He could bear any trial, perform any duty, subdue any evil, and conquer any temptation. Paul says that as long as we are in Christ, we can accomplish anything Christ can accomplish through us. However, the opposite is equally true: without Christ, we can accomplish nothing. Jesus said, *"I am the vine, ye are the branches: He that abideth in me, and I in him, the same bringeth forth much fruit: for without me ye can do nothing"* (John 15:5).

Our homes and marriages are being destroyed because people think they can make it work without Christ. He didn't say, "Without me ye can do very little." He said, *"without me ye can do nothing."*

Paul said, "Don't think that I am doing what I am doing just because I am a good man." It had nothing to do with Paul being a good man. Good men fall into sin every day. It had everything to do with Paul allowing Christ to work through Him to defeat Satan in his life.

More than ever before, we need to keep ourselves clean and pure. We start by controlling what we think about. We must avoid letting Satan build strongholds in our minds that will hinder us from having the victory God wants us to have in our lives.

"What are some strongholds Satan wants to use in my mind," you ask? That is the subject of the next chapter.

# CHAPTER 3

# One, Two, Three...
# The Devil's After Me

I remember the little song I was taught as a child that said, "One, two, three, the Devil's after me. Four, five, six, he's always throwing sticks. Seven, eight, nine, he missed me every time. Hallelujah! Hallelujah! I'm saved."

Well, it is true; the Devil *is* after you! But he is not just throwing sticks at you. He has an entire arsenal of weapons he has built to use and he prides himself in knowing which weapon of his will get the job done. Just as a fisherman uses different bait for different types of fish, Satan knows which temptation works best for different people. He has been at this for a long time so he knows what he is doing.

You and I might be idle, but Satan is not. We may take some time off, but Satan never takes a vacation. He is always on the lookout for his next victim. In fact, the Bible tells us of the time when Satan went after one of his biggest targets. His name was Job.

*And the LORD said unto Satan, Whence comest thou? Then Satan answered the LORD, and said, From going to and fro in the earth, and from walking up and down in it. And the LORD said unto Satan, Hast thou **considered** my servant Job, that **there is none like him** in the earth, a perfect and an upright man, one that feareth God, and escheweth evil? (Job 1:7-8)*

What a testimony Job must have had for God to be able to offer him up to Satan as an example of a *"perfect and an upright man."* In fact, God went so far as to say that *"there is none like him in the earth."* You can be sure Satan will consider anyone who is a true servant of God, but especially if there is *"none like him."*

It is evident that Job's life and character intrigued Satan. What was it about Job that caused him to have an undying loyalty to a God whom he could not see? This must have been a mystery to Satan. I am sure that after God asked Satan if he had considered Job, he thought to himself, "Not yet, but I will consider him now."

I have no doubt that when he began to consider Job's life; he thoroughly investigated it as carefully and methodically as a thief would case a house when he is planning to rob it. A thief will take note of every window and door. He will know if there is an alarm system and how to disarm it. He will even observe the schedule of the occupants to know when they will be away from the house leaving it unprotected. Satan is the ultimate thief. He not only **knows** every trick of the trade; he *invented* them!

When Satan began looking at the life of Job, he took note of all Job had. "Let's see," he said to himself, "he owns camels, oxen and many other animals. I can take those away. Oh, and I must not forget his health. If I can afflict him physically, that would also be devastating to him."

"Then," he thought, "he has three daughters and seven sons. If I can destroy them, it would really devastate the mind of Job. If I could bury his mind in the pits of depression, that would get him."

"Finally," he said, "I will use his wife against him. Surely that would do him in and make him question God." And that is exactly what he did. A man can face a lot of difficult circumstances in life as long as he has the support of his wife. What an encouragement a godly wife can be in difficult times as she reminds her husband to keep trusting God. Of all the things Job lost, probably the greatest loss was the support of his wife. Nothing could have hurt him worse than to hear her say to him, "Job, why don't you just curse God and die?"

Some say that a crisis makes the man. But a crisis does not **make** a man; it only reveals what a man is already made of. Satan learned the reason God had offered him Job to begin with. He was seeing what Job was made of. The more he began to try Job, the more he realize there truly was *"none like him."*

The verses following Job's losses reveal the kind of man Satan was dealing with. The Bible says, *"Then Job arose, and rent his mantle, and shaved his head, and fell down upon the ground, and worshipped"* (Job 1:20). What? Did I read that right? It says that after all Job faced and after all he lost, he fell down and worshipped God! That must have really stumped Satan.

Job went on to say in the next verse, *"Naked came I out of my mother's womb, and naked shall I return thither: the LORD gave, and the LORD hath taken away; blessed be the name of the LORD"* (v.21). I can hear Satan saying to himself, "Now this **really** doesn't make any sense to me."

But the last verse is probably the most telling. *"In all this Job sinned not, nor charged God foolishly"* (v.22). That was exactly what Satan was trying to get him to do. He wanted Job to foolishly accuse God of being unloving and unfair, but he never did.

## A Lesson Learned

What can we learn from Satan's attack on Job? The higher we go with God, the fiercer Satan's attacks become. As someone once put it, "New levels; new devils." Satan is always on the lookout for those whom he knows are God's choicest servants. Not only does he watch them, but he no doubt assigns his choicest demons to take careful aim at them and hopefully knock them down.

He has traps that have been carefully placed and snares that are ready to trap us if we are not careful. This is especially true for leaders in the church. That is why Paul wrote to Timothy that a pastor *"...must have a good report of them which are without; lest he fall into reproach and the snare of the devil"* (1 Tim. 3:7).

The title of this chapter *"One, Two Three...The Devil's After Me,"* is not meant to imply that it is Satan himself who is after us. The Bible teaches that God is omnipresent (everywhere at once), but Satan is not. The way Satan accomplishes his work is by not acting alone.

Few of us have been tempted directly by Satan himself. He has an entire host of inferior spirits under his control. Just as God has His faithful servants, Satan also has his evil cohorts to do his bidding; those whom he sends to hinder God's work.

Paul encountered this satanic opposition on more than one occasion.

*But Elymas the sorcerer (for so is his name by interpretation) withstood them, seeking to turn away the deputy from the faith. Then Saul, (who also is called Paul,) filled with the Holy Ghost, set his eyes on him, And said, O full of all subtilty and all mischief, thou child of the devil, thou enemy of all righteousness, wilt thou not cease to pervert the right ways of the Lord? (Acts 13:8-10)*

*Wherefore we would have come unto you, even I Paul, once and again; but Satan hindered us. (1 Thess. 2:18)*

Scripture teaches that there are people sent by Satan to hinder God's work. The Apostle Paul calls them *"...false apostles, deceitful workers, transforming themselves into the apostles of Christ. And no marvel; for Satan himself is transformed into an angel of light. Therefore it is no great thing if his ministers also be transformed as the ministers of righteousness; whose end shall be according to their works"* (2 Cor. 11:13-15).

So it should not surprise us that Satan would send his minions to attack us, too. Spurgeon said, "As birds peck at the ripest fruit, so may you expect Satan to be most busy against you." He went on to say, "Beloved friend, the Archenemy wants to make you wretched here if he cannot have you hereafter."

## Trick or Trick?

No, that is not a typo. "Shouldn't it be trick or treat," you ask? No, because when it comes to Satan, all you will ever get is tricked. He offers no real treats. The Bible says, *"Lest Satan should get an advantage of us: for we are not ignorant of his devices"* (2 Cor. 2:11).

The word *"devices"* means "thoughts, tricks, or temptations." Dr. Jon Jenkins, in his book, *The Truth About Temptation,* said, "As long as we are ignorant, Satan will be triumphant. The subject of spiritual warfare is both foreign and frightening because of the ignorance of God's people." Over and over, the Apostle Paul said that we are not to be ignorant when it comes to the way Satan works.

One day I received a phone call from a person who identified himself as being a representative from my credit card company. He said there were some errors with my account and, to correct the errors, he needed me to give him my credit card number and personal information. A red flag immediately went up!

I said to him, "If you are truly with the credit card company, you would already know what my credit card number is." Click. All I heard was a dial-tone. He was trying to scam me and had been found out! Sadly, I've heard of many elderly people who lost their life's savings because they fell to such a scam.

Satan is nothing but one big scam artist who is out to scam you and me. Jesus said, *"He was a murderer from the beginning, and abode not in the truth, because there is no truth in him. When he speaketh a lie, he speaketh of his own: for he is a liar, and the father of it"* (John 8:44).

He is out to convince us that God doesn't love us and that He is not worthy of our trust. But we must remember that *"there is no truth in him."* Everything he says is a lie because *"he is a liar, and the father of it."*

When we listen to his lies, we are allowing him to *"get an advantage of us"* (2 Cor. 2:11).

## A Wicked Welcome Mat

Usually a scam artist cannot get your information unless you give it to them. Likewise, Satan cannot deceive us and trick us unless we allow him to do so. Paul tells us not to *"give place to the devil"* (Eph. 4:27).

Because some have given place to the devil, many have been led into false doctrine and even into cults. The Bible gives us a specific warning to heed.

> *"Now the Spirit speaketh expressly, that in the latter times some shall depart from the faith, giving heed to seducing spirits, and doctrines of devils;" (1 Tim. 4:1)*

Notice they depart from the faith and are led into believing the doctrines of devils because they are *"giving heed to"* these *"seducing spirits."*

The words *"giving heed to"* means "to pay attention to" or "to be cautious about." In other words, the Bible is saying that a person can be led away into false doctrine and away from God simply by not being cautious or paying attention to the things they are allowing to influence them.

When you allow things into your life that are not under God's control, you are literally laying out a wicked welcome mat at the front door of your heart and mind for Satan to enter at will.

## A Rusty Old Cage

Paul Harvey once told the story that S. D. Gordon, a Boston preacher, used a beat-up rusty bird cage one Sunday to illustrate his sermon. First he explained how he had come by the cage, saying when he first saw it, it contained several miserable small birds, and was carried by a boy of about ten.

Curious, he asked the boy what he was going to do with the birds, which he had obviously trapped. "I'm going to play with them and have some fun with them," the boy responded. "But after that?" the preacher persisted. "Oh, I have some cats at home, and they like birds," said the boy.

Compassion tugged at the minister's heart, and he asked the boy what he would take for the birds. Surprised, the boy blurted: "Mister, you don't want to buy these birds. They're ugly; just field birds. They don't sing, or anything." Nevertheless, Dr. Gordon persisted, and soon struck a bargain with the boy for the birds. At the first opportunity he released the poor creatures.

After explaining the presence of the empty cage, Dr. Gordon then told another story: this time about how Satan boasted that he had baited a trap and caught a world full of people. "What are you going to do with them?" Jesus asked him. "I'm going to play with them, tease them; make them marry and divorce, and fight and kill one another. I'll teach them to throw bombs at each other," Satan replied. "And when you get tired of playing with them, what will you do with them?" Jesus asked. "Condemn them," Satan answered. "They're no good anyway."

Jesus then asked what Satan would take for them. "You can't be serious," the devil responded. "They would just spit on You. They'd hit you and hammer nails into You. They're no good." "How much?" the Lord asked again. "All your tears and all your blood; that's the price," Satan said gleefully.

Jesus paid the price, took the cage, and opened the door! I am so thankful that the Bible says Jesus came to free us from the bondage of sin and *"If the Son therefore shall make you free, ye shall be free indeed"* (John 8:36).

# CHAPTER 4

# Mind Games

*Watch your thoughts; they become words.*

*Watch your words; they become actions.*

*Watch your actions; they become habits.*

*Watch your habits; they become character.*

*Watch your character; it becomes your destiny.*

If you have ever played sports, you have probably been a victim of mind games. Mind games are something a player will use, hoping to gain an advantage by getting into the head of their opponent. It is also called psyching someone out. You wouldn't think it would be a big deal, but many sports teams have actually defeated themselves because they allowed their opponent to beat them mentally.

A great example of this is in one of my favorite scenes from the movie *The Hoosiers*. A little high school basketball team from the rural town of Hickory, Indiana, shocks everyone by reaching the state championship game.

It is their first time playing in a large arena and before a crowd bigger than any they've seen. The Hickory players were up against a team from South Bend, whose players were taller and more athletic. As they walked into the enormous arena for the first time, you could tell they were already setting themselves up mentally to fail. This court was too big. The opponent was too tough.

Their coach saw what was happening and gave them a tape measure. He made them measure the height of the goal rim. Then he made them measure the distance to the free throw line. He was driving home the fact that this court and basketball goal were no bigger than the one they played on back home. He wanted them to realize that they could win in the big arena as easily as they had won in any of the other places that had played.

Satan loves to play mind games. He knows that if he can get in our heads, he can defeat us before we even get started.

Controlling your thought life is so important because your thoughts can have an incredible impact on your actions. They also have an incredible impact on the direction your life will take. Some say, "You are what you eat." But the Bible says, "You are what you think." Remember, Proverbs 23:7 says, *"...as he thinketh in his heart, so is he:"* Satan knows this and has a special arsenal of weapons designed to attack our minds in many different ways.

While Satan does have the power to attack our minds, he cannot force us to give in to his assault. If we choose to surrender our thought life to him, we are still accountable. The Bible says that at the judgment, God *"...will bring to light the hidden things of darkness, and will make manifest the counsels of the hearts:"* (1 Cor. 4:5).

What a scary thought, that one day God will expose what we think about! No wonder the psalmist prayed, *"Let the words of my mouth, and the meditation of my heart, be acceptable in thy sight, O LORD, my strength, and my redeemer"* (Ps. 19:14). Can you say that the words you speak are pleasing to God? Can you say that the things you think about are pleasing to God? Convicting, isn't it?

Since we are accountable for what we think, we need to be aware of the various ways Satan may choose to launch an attack against our minds. While there are many weapons Satan uses, I will mention only a few.

## WEAPON #1 – DISCOURAGEMENT

In 1 Kings 18, Elijah experienced a great spiritual victory. He won a face-to-face confrontation with eight hundred and fifty prophets of Baal, proving that he served the one true God. This was one of the greatest spiritual victories he had ever experienced in his ministry.

When word got back to the wicked Queen Jezebel, she sent a message to him saying, "Elijah, by tomorrow I will make sure you are like the prophets you just killed." His great victory was short-lived. He was already facing opposition from Satan.

You need to realize that any time you take a stand for God and make progress for Him, Satan will begin attacking you. So, Elijah got scared and fled to the wilderness. Imagine: the great Elijah that stood boldly against eight hundred and fifty false prophets is now running from one woman!

When we see him again, he is sitting under a juniper tree, defeated, discouraged, and disillusioned with the whole situation.

Why was he being threatened? Had he not done the right thing up on Mount Carmel?

Understand that it wasn't his circumstances or what Jezebel said to him that had gotten him discouraged. It was what he THOUGHT about his circumstances that got him discouraged. His thoughts were defeating him more than what was happening around him.

## Messed Up Thinking

Satan could not stop Elijah from having a great victory, but he messed up his thinking to the point that he could not enjoy his victory. As believers, the Bible says in 1 Corinthians 15:57 that we have victory through Jesus Christ right now: *"But thanks be to God, which giveth us the victory through our Lord Jesus Christ."*

Satan cannot take away our victory in Jesus Christ, but we can allow him to ruin our thinking so that we cannot enjoy a victorious life. The devil majors on negative thinking. He loves to get believers thinking like unbelievers.

Someone said that when trials and opposition comes, many Christians come down with a mild case of atheism.

They are saved people, but they are thinking like lost people. They believe in God, but they think like an atheist! They know there is a God, but doubt that He is really in control of their situation.

Isn't it funny how we can trust God for the biggest thing of all, saving our soul, but we have a difficult time trusting Him in lesser matters? What took place when you got saved was the greatest miracle you will ever experience. If you can trust God with your eternity, you can definitely trust Him with anything that happens in *this* life.

That is what Paul told Timothy in 2 Timothy 1:12, *"I know whom I have believed, and am persuaded that he is able to keep that which I have committed unto him against that day."* If you can commit your SOUL to Him, you can commit your CIRCUMSTANCES to Him.

## It's A State Of Mind

Discouragement is a state of mind, not a set of circumstances. We know this is true because in all walks of life we see people who were able to overcome extremely negative circumstances and live victorious lives.

One such person was Bethany Hamilton. Born into a family of surfers on the island of Kauai, Hawaii, Bethany began surfing at a young age. At the age of eight, she entered her first surf competition. At the age of thirteen, the unthinkable happened: Bethany was attacked by a 14-foot tiger shark while surfing off Kauai's North Shore.

The attack left Bethany with a severed left arm, and by all accounts her surfing career was over. She would never surf again. But even after losing a lot of blood, and making it through several surgeries without infection, Bethany not only began to recover, but did so with an unbelievably positive attitude.

Miraculously, just one month after the attack, Bethany returned to the water to continue pursuing her goal to become a professional surfer. In January of 2004, Bethany made her return to surf competition, placing 5th in the Open Women's division of that contest. Just over a year after the attack, she took 1st place in the Explorer Women's division of the 2005 NSSA National Championships—winning her first National Title.

She could have easily given up while lying in that hospital room. She could have let thoughts of doubt and fear lead her into a pit of discouragement and depression that could have completely altered the course of her life. But she didn't! Her positive outlook helped bring her back.

Your circumstances will not cause you to be discouraged, but your THOUGHTS about your circumstances will. If you let Satan get into your head, he will play mind games with you and defeat you every time.

Again, the Bible says that we are what we think. If I think defeated thoughts, I will be defeated. If I think negative thoughts, I will become negative. If, on the other hand, I think encouraging thoughts, I will become encouraged.

## Think Happy Thoughts

We even see this in the life of Paul. In Acts 26, he had been arrested and brought before the king to answer for the charges brought against him. It didn't look very good; the circumstances were against him. The judicial system was against him. There was really no reason for him to be encouraged with the situation whatsoever. But when the king let him speak, he said, *"I think myself happy, king Agrippa, because I shall answer for myself this day before thee touching all the things whereof I am accused of the Jews"* (Acts 26:2).

He could have said, "This is not fair. I am being railroaded here." He could have said, "I want my lawyer!" But instead he said, *"I think myself happy."*

One thing that stands out among the great giants of the faith is not that they faced no difficult circumstances, because we know they did. What stands out is the fact that they learned how to stay encouraged even in the most discouraging situations.

One problem many people have is that their happiness depends upon other people or upon better circumstances. They never seem to be in control of their own attitude. But when we allow our happiness to depend upon others, we will most likely stay in a valley of discouragement.

David, a man who often had more enemies than friends, did not leave his encouragement to chance. Even in the most stressful of situations, he learned how to encourage himself in the Lord.

*"And David was greatly distressed; for the people spake of stoning him, because the soul of all the people was grieved, every man for his sons and for his daughters: but David encouraged himself in the LORD his God." (1 Samuel 30:6)*

The people were saying they wanted to stone David. These were discouraging circumstances to say the least! No wonder David was greatly distressed. He had every right to be discouraged, but he didn't let himself stay that way.

What did he do? Did he sit in the corner crying because there was no one to encourage him? No. The

Bible says *"David encouraged himself in the LORD his God."* He could have tried to get encouragement through many different ways, but he realized the best way was to encourage himself *"in the LORD his God."*

Jesus said in John 16:33, *"These things I have spoken unto you, that in me ye might have peace. In the world ye shall have tribulation: but be of good cheer; I have overcome the world."* Notice that peace does not come from circumstances. Jesus said, *"in me ye might have peace."* True peace comes only from Jesus.

He then says that while we are living in this world, we will have tribulations. Boy, that is encouraging, isn't it? Well, actually, He says we SHOULD be encouraged. *"But be of good cheer,"* He said. How? How can we be happy while going through tribulations? "Ah," he said. "That's easy. You can be happy because I have already overcome the world." And since the Overcomer lives within us, we can overcome, too!

## WEAPON #2 – WORRY

One of the most destructive habits is also so common that many consider it as natural as breathing and as harmless as blinking. That habit is called worry. It is such a deceptive thief that its victims don't even know they've been robbed...of peace, of joy, of their time, and of emotional well-being.

## *What Is Worry?*

In the New Testament, one Greek word translated as "worry" is *merimnao*, which means "to be anxious; to be distracted" or "to have a divided mind." To worry is to divide your mind between that which is useful and worthwhile and that which is damaging and destructive.

Jesus spoke of worrying in Matthew 6:27 when he said, *"Which of you by taking thought can add one cubit unto his stature?"* In other words, all the worrying in the world cannot change your stature or your situation in the least.

To begin with, let me say that there is hope! The very fact that Jesus Himself spoke about worry means that there are answers from God for your problem. We do not have to rely on man's opinions or ideas. As a believer, you have God's Word to teach you how to handle worry.

In Matthew 6, Jesus is speaking about worry. The encouraging thing is that He was speaking to His own followers! That should give you hope. Why? Because, if nothing else, it assures you that even believers can and do struggle with worry.

## *Worry Is Sinful*

What does Jesus say about worry? In Matthew 6, He tells us no fewer than three times that it is wrong. Paul says the same thing in Philippians 4:6 when he said, *"Be careful for nothing;"*

Someone might ask, "If worry is so common, why is it sinful? Besides, doesn't it show that we are concerned about things in life? Isn't it better to worry a little than to be indifferent to the world around us?"

Jesus answers these questions in Matthew, chapter 6. He not only says it is wrong; He gives us reasons why it is wrong. Worry is wrong because its underlying nature is:

***Disbelief***—Worry reveals that you really don't believe God when He says He will provide all that you need. Worry is basically a negative view of the future. If you are a worrier, you are spending time speculating on what may or may not happen and then fearing the worst. Jesus tells us:

> *Therefore I say unto you, Take no thought for your life, what ye shall eat, or what ye shall drink; nor yet for your body, what ye shall put on. Is not the life more than meat, and the body than raiment?* ***26*** *Behold the fowls of the air: for they sow not, neither do they reap, nor gather into barns; yet your heavenly Father feedeth them. Are ye not much better than they?* ***27*** *Which of you by taking thought can add one cubit unto his stature?* ***28*** *And why take ye thought*

*for raiment? Consider the lilies of the field, how they grow; they toil not, neither do they spin: **29** And yet I say unto you, That even Solomon in all his glory was not arrayed like one of these. **30** Wherefore, if God so clothe the grass of the field, which to day is, and to morrow is cast into the oven, shall he not much more clothe you, O ye of little faith? (Matthew 6:25-30)*

Disbelief ultimately stems from a lack of faith. As unbelief gets the upper hand in our hearts, the result is anxiety. So the antidote to worry is to trust in God.

***Disobedience***—When you worry, it shows that you are taking on personal responsibility and concern for that which God has already promised to provide.

*Therefore take no thought, saying, What shall we eat? or, What shall we drink? or, Wherewithal shall we be clothed? (For after all these things do the Gentiles seek:) for your heavenly Father knoweth that ye have need of all these things. But seek ye first the kingdom of God, and his righteousness; and all these things shall be added unto you. (Matt. 6:31-33)*

Worry often causes us to act in disobedience by trying to obtain (our way) the things God promised to supply.

***Destruction***—Worry destroys your physical body, which is the temple of the Holy Spirit. Paul said in 1 Corinthians 6:19-20, *"What? know ye not that your body is the temple of the Holy Ghost which is in you, which ye have of God, and ye are not your own? For ye are bought with a price: therefore glorify God in your body, and in your spirit, which are God's."*

Worry is physically destructive because it can bring about a host of physical ailments, such as high blood pressure, heart trouble, headaches, and stomach disorders.

***Dishonor***—Worry shifts the focus of attention from the all sufficient power of Christ to your human insufficiency and insecurity. Ultimately, worry can undermine your Christian witness by presenting God as powerless and unworthy of praise.

The Bible says, *"Let your light so shine before men, that they may see your good works, and glorify your Father which is in heaven"* (Matt. 5:16).

## WEAPON #3 – GUILT

Are you battling with guilt? Is it **good** guilt or **bad** guilt? "What? Good guilt? I never knew there was such a thing as good guilt," you say. "What is the difference between good guilt and bad guilt?"

Good guilt is godly guilt. It is a loving tool of God used to convict, correct, and conform your character when you go astray. Bad guilt is used by Satan that will overshadow you with feelings of shame and condemnation. Godly guilt is your friend. Godly guilt motivates you to repent and be free from your sin. But false guilt is a relentless foe. It is the enemy within that encourages not godly, but superficial sorrow that brings death!

Paul spoke of this in 2 Corinthians 7:9-10:

*"Now I rejoice, not that ye were made sorry, but that ye sorrowed to repentance: for ye were made sorry after a godly manner...For godly sorrow worketh repentance to salvation not to be repented of: but the sorrow of the world worketh death."*

## What Is True Guilt?

From earliest childhood, no one has escaped guilt. We experienced guilt when we stole a cookie or told a lie. True guilt is the result of sin. When we sin we are guilty, and a penalty must be paid for our sin so that fellowship with God can be restored.

After David committed adultery with Bathsheba, he repented and cried out to God, *"Against thee, thee only, have I sinned, and done this evil in thy sight"* (Ps. 51:4). Sin is first and foremost a sin against God and guilt is therefore a result of that sin. James 2:10 says, *"For whosoever shall keep the whole law, and yet offend in one point, he is guilty of all."*

## How Should I Respond To Guilt?

Begin by confessing any sin. You experience true guilt when you recognize the fact that you have sinned. David was honest about his sin in Psalm 32:5: *"I acknowledged my sin unto thee, and mine iniquity have I not hid. I said, I will confess my transgressions unto the LORD; and thou forgavest the iniquity of my sin. Selah."*

How did God respond? He forgave David's sin and the good news is His response is the same for anyone who will confess their sin to Him. The Bible says in 1 John 1:9, *"If we confess our sins, he is faithful and just to forgive us our sins, and to cleanse us from all unrighteousness."*

When the sin goes away, so does the guilt. In fact, the Bible says that when God forgives your sin, he removes it *"As far as the east is from the west"* (Ps. 103:12).

## WEAPON #4 – ANGER

Will Rogers said, "People who fly into a rage seldom make a good landing!" The Bible says, *"He that is soon angry dealeth foolishly: and a man of wicked devices is hated."* (Prov. 14:17).

Did you know that nothing good can come from a bad temper? James 1:20 says, *"For the wrath of man worketh not the righteousness of God."*

Someone defined anger as "A sudden explosion of madness." An angry man picks a fight. But a man in control of his anger stops a fight. *"A wrathful man stirreth up strife: but he that is slow to anger appeaseth strife"* (Prov. 15:18). An angry man stirs up strife in the home. He stirs up strife in the church. He basically stirs up trouble wherever he goes because wherever he goes, he takes his anger with him.

Proverbs 25:8 says, *"Go not forth hastily to strive, lest thou know not what to do in the end thereof, when thy neighbour hath put thee to shame."*

Notice the first part of that verse again. It says, *"Go not forth hastily to strive."* God says to be careful about having a short fuse and a quick temper. The next part says, *"...when thy neighbour hath put thee to shame."* Your neighbor knows you best. In fact, the closest neighbor you have is your spouse and family. No one lives any closer to you than they do. They see you when no one else does.

Proverbs 29:20 says, *"Seest thou a man that is hasty in his words? there is more hope of a fool than of him."* If there's one thing that really gets us into trouble it is being hasty with our words. You know that feeling that wells up inside you when you get angry and makes you want to tell someone off? The Bible says, it would be better for you to not say anything right then out of anger or you will say the wrong thing.

If you have a problem with anger, here are some things to do.

## Confess It

Admit you have a problem with anger. Own up to it. But that is not all. Proverbs 29:22 says, *"An angry man stirreth up strife, and a furious man aboundeth in transgression."* Now, we've already seen that *"An angry man stirreth up strife,"* but this goes a step further. It has been said that when a person loses his temper, there is more to it than just what he is angry about. That is what the Bible is saying here: *"a furious man aboundeth in transgression."*

See, it is a domino effect. There are other sins in this man's life than just anger. When a man gets angry and loses his temper at his wife because his toast is a little burnt, the toast is NOT the real issue there. There is more than meets the eye that has been simmering under the surface.

Since the Bible says that an angry man literally *"abounds"* in transgressions, there are probably others sins that need to be dealt with before the anger will be resolved. 1 John 1:8, says, *"If we say that we have no sin, we deceive ourselves, and the truth is not in us."*

## Consider It

Proverbs 25:28 says, *"He that hath no rule over his own spirit is like a city that is broken down, and without walls."* A city that is without walls is without protection. They must consider what the lack of protection is doing to them and their families.

Likewise, an angry man must consider what harm his anger is doing to himself, his family, and his relationship with God.

## Control It

Proverbs 29:11 says, *"A fool uttereth all his mind: but a wise man keepeth it in till afterwards."* Some people will give you a piece of their mind and they usually don't have much to spare!

They say, "Well I just speak my mind." That's not always a good thing. Remember the old saying: "It is better to keep your mouth shut and be thought a fool, than to open your mouth and remove all doubt!"

The last part of that verse says, *"a wise man keepeth it in till afterwards."* I can't tell you how many times that just waiting a while before responding to something has saved me considerable embarrassment. That is scriptural. You shouldn't utter all of your mind. You wait until you have calmed down and can think straight.

"Well, I just can't control my anger, preacher." sure you can. I can prove it. You get into a big argument and you raise your voice in anger then all the sudden the phone rings and you say in a calm voice, "Hello? Hi, preacher! Why we were just sitting her re-enacting the Sermon on the Mount. Honey, you can get down off the table now." What did you do? You instantly controlled your so-called uncontrollable temper.

One of the best ways to avoid having a problem with anger is by not becoming friends with a person who has a problem with anger. Because the Bible teaches us that our friends will influence our behavior.

*Make no friendship with an angry man; and with a furious man thou shalt not go: Lest thou learn his ways, and get a snare to thy soul. (Prov. 22:24-25)*

## That's not all, folks!

This is not all of Satan's weapons. These were just a few that he will use against your mind. In 2 Corinthians chapter ten, Paul gives us three things to keep in mind the next time Satan begins to attack us.

**We must fight the flesh with the Spirit.** In verse 3 Paul wrote, *"For though we walk in the flesh, we do not war after the flesh:"* In other words, our weapons are not fleshly weapons.

Many times we fail to control our thought lives because we try to fight the flesh with the flesh. We will never conquer our flesh using the world's methods. David said in Psalm 1:1-2, *"Blessed is the man that walketh not in the counsel of the ungodly, nor standeth in the way of sinners, nor sitteth in the seat of the scornful. But his delight is in the law of the LORD; and in his law doth he meditate day and night."* In other words, the *"blessed"* or happy man is one who meditates on spiritual things, *"the law of the LORD."*

**We must trust God's power to pull down the strongholds.** In verse 4, Paul said, *"For the weapons of our warfare are not carnal, but mighty through God to the pulling down of strong holds;"*

While we are no match for the power of Satan by ourselves, he is no match for the power of God! Paul reminds us that we can accomplish anything through God's power. He said, *"I can do all things through Christ which strengtheneth me"* (Phil. 4:13)

**We must reject (cast down) any thought that leads us to doubt God or His Word.** Verse five says, *"Casting down imaginations, and every high thing that* *exalteth itself against the knowledge of God..."* Though we have access to God's power, we are still responsible for rejecting the wrong thoughts ourselves.

That is our responsibility. Any thought that would cause us to doubt God or his Word must be rejected.

**We must bring every thought captive by obeying Jesus Christ.** Paul goes on to say in the second half of verse five, *"...and bringing into captivity every thought to the obedience of Christ;"*

One of the best ways to avoid doing what is wrong is by doing what is right. In other words, the best way to guard against disobedience is through active obedience. If you want to be victorious in defeating Satan's attacks on you, begin reading God's Word and obeying what it says.

# CHAPTER 5

# Mind Control

In 1838 on the Island of Jamaica, a man named William Knibb, who was an English Baptist minister and missionary to Jamaica, gathered thousands of slaves together for a celebration. They were celebrating the New Emancipation Proclamation Act that would abolish slavery on the island. They built an immense coffin and placed into it chains, branding irons, fetters of all kinds, slave garments and anything else that represented the terrible slavery system that was now coming to a welcome end.

At the stroke of the midnight bell, Knibb shouted out, "The monster is dying." Soon, thousands of voices united together shouting, "The monster is dead, the monster is dead, let us bury him." They shut the coffin lid and lowered it into a huge grave and covered it up. That night, thousands of voices grew hoarse, shouting and crying with joy because they once were in bondage to slavery, but now they were free.

Sadly, the story does not end there. There is a tragic side. While many rejoiced in their new liberty and freedom, there were some slaves that lived in remote areas of the island. These slaves did not know they had legally been set free. Because they had never been informed of the law, they still continued to serve their slave masters. Their former masters successfully kept the news from them as long as they could. By law they had been declared free men and did not have to live as slaves any longer. However, ignorance of the truth kept them in bondage.

As tragic as that story is, let me tell you an even sadder story. The same type of thing is happening spiritually in our day. Jesus Christ, because of his death, burial, and resurrection, has issued an Emancipation Proclamation of liberty and freedom from sin to everyone who will receive Him. But like some of the Jamaicans were, there are those today that just don't understand that they no longer have to live as slaves to sin. They do not have to let Satan control their minds.

The battle for the mind is really a battle for mind control. The question is who is going to control yours? We saw in chapter 2 that Satan is an INVISIBLE enemy but, thankfully, he is not an INVINCIBLE enemy! God has not left us defenseless. Through God's Word we have the capability of being more protected than a S.W.A.T. Team! The armor God gives us is backed by His power, and nothing can penetrate that.

God Word promises us that *"There hath no temptation taken you but such as is common to man: but God is faithful, who will not suffer you to be tempted above that ye are able; but will with the temptation also make a way to escape, that ye may be able to bear it"* (1 Cor. 10:13).

If you are tempted to think sinful thoughts, congratulations! You are normal! But just because it is normal to face temptation doesn't mean we can use that as an excuse to give in to it.

The Bible doesn't say that with the temptation He will also make "a way of excuse." It says He will make *"a way to escape."* Big difference! Many fall to temptation because they never even tried to escape it to begin with. Someone said, "When fleeing temptation, never leave a forwarding address."

In Ephesians chapter 6, Paul gives us the armor we need to put on if we are going to gain control of our minds. We need the right protection because every morning we wake up we're in a battle, a battle for mind control.

## Paul says, "Strengthen up!"

Before a boxer ever enters the ring to face his opponent, he has put himself through rigorous strength training. While everyone else is playing, he is preparing. While everyone else is relaxing, he is relentless; training smarter and working out harder so that he will not fall when he is in the ring.

As Christians, we should take our bout with Satan just as seriously. Paul tells us we should strengthen ourselves up, but we can't rely upon OUR strength. He said, *"Finally, my brethren, be strong in the Lord, and in the power of his might"* (Eph. 6:10).

Very few Christians are actually living in the power of *His* might. They live with a defeatist attitude as if God is not in control and the Bible isn't true! When someone begins living that kind of life, one of two things is true: they have quit reading the Bible or they do not believe what they **do** read!

Some say, "I just can't get victory over this." One reason might be because you don't BELIEVE you can have victory. 2 Timothy 1:7 says, *"For God hath not given us the spirit of fear; but of power, and of love, and of a sound mind."* God has the power to help us be victorious.

You might not see the victory yet. You might not feel the victory, yet. But by faith, claim the victory we have already been given in Christ. Don't keep ASKING for victory, start ACTING in Victory! When we ask for victory, we are asking for something we have already been given.

> *"But thanks be to God, which giveth us the victory through our Lord Jesus Christ. Therefore, my beloved brethren, be ye stedfast, unmoveable, always abounding in the work of the Lord, forasmuch as ye know that your labour is not in vain in the Lord." (1 Cor. 15:57-58)*

## Paul says, "Stand up!"

The next thing Paul tells us to do is to *"Stand therefore, having your loins girt about with truth"* (v.14). He says, "Because you are living in an evil day and are facing an evil enemy, you need to stand therefore."

A boxer cannot win a match by lying on the mat. He must be the last one standing. More than ever before, we need God's people to take a stand. America is in the shape she is in, in part, because God's people have been too quiet. The world is standing up for what **they** want more than God's people are standing up for what **He** wants.

"What do I do, preacher, when temptation comes my way?" STAND! It doesn't take money to stand. It doesn't take talent to stand. It doesn't take popularity to stand. Anyone can stand. Even a lifeless mannequin in the department store can stand!

## Paul says, "Suit Up!"

How do we do this? By putting on the whole armor of God. Ephesians 4:11 says, *"Put on the whole armour of God, that ye may be able to stand against the wiles of the devil."*

We not only need the WHOLE armor of God; we need the HOLY armor of God. So what exactly is the armor of God we are to put on? Paul gives us a detail list of what all is included in the armor we need.

### The Girdle or Belt of Truth

How are we to stand? Paul says to stand *"having your loins girt about with truth."* We need the girdle of truth. This girdle (or belt) is to protect us. Since Satan is the father of lies and the Bible says *"there is no truth in him"* (John 8:44), we must fight his lies and the best way to combat lies is with the truth!

Truth speaks of integrity so this girdle will protect our integrity. If you are going to win the war of your mind, then you are going to need integrity.

We cannot live a life that's dishonest. Too many of God's people are living a lie; they are living a dishonest life. They are one way at church but live a different way everywhere else. So, when the Bible speaks of putting on the girdle of truth, it is speaking of putting on a belt of integrity. If there is one thing we need in our lives, it is integrity.

We need to keep this belt on tight, because if this belt comes loose, everything else falls apart. When a person's integrity goes, everything else goes with it. You can't trust a person who has no integrity.

**You need integrity in your MARRIAGE.** Many spouses can't trust each other. Whether it is due to an unfaithful act or simply a lack of character, many marriages are hurting due to a lack of trust which is the result of a lack of integrity.

**You need integrity in your FAMILY.** Many parents have lost integrity because they will say "no" to their children sometimes, then turn around and allow what they had previously said "no" to. Their children grow up without much integrity because they see the lack of integrity in the lives of their parents.

**You need integrity at WORK.** Paul tells us in Ephesians 4:1 that our true vocation is to serve Jesus Christ. No matter where you work or what your position may be, your first calling is to live a life of integrity for Jesus Christ. Many employees have been asked by their employers to do something unethical, it is in those situations that you and I will need the integrity to take a stand for what is right no matter the cost.

**We need integrity at CHURCH.** Countless churches have begun to decay from the inside because they have people in leadership positions with no integrity. It is no surprise why these churches are dead spiritually. Paul said, *"For to be carnally minded is death; but to be spiritually minded is life and peace"* (Rom. 8:6).

So, we see that integrity is important to every aspect of our lives. Every day you need to put on the belt of integrity.

In the Bible days, the girdle was an important part of their dress in war as well as in peace. Since they wore loose, flowing robes, it became necessary to gird them up as they traveled or as they labored.

70

The girdle (or belt) was sometimes made of iron or steel and was designed to keep every part of the armor in its place.

That is what truth and integrity does for us. Without truth, none of the rest of the armor matters!

"How do I put on integrity," you ask? Here's how you can do it. Every day ask yourself this question: "Am I living the life of a Christian? Am I really being honest in my Christian walk?"

## The Breastplate of Righteousness

The next thing we need to put on is *"the breastplate of righteousness;"* (Eph. 6:14). The word *"righteousness"* means "right living." When telling us how to show we are faithful servants of God, he says we show *"By the word of truth, by the power of God, by the armour of righteousness on the right hand and on the left,"* (2 Cor. 6:7).

If the girdle of truth represents INTEGRITY, then the breastplate of righteousness represents PURITY. The breastplate would protect the soldier's vital organs and the breastplate of righteousness will protect our vital organs, too! There is nothing more vital to the Christian life than INTEGRITY and PURITY! Proverbs 4:23 says, *"Keep thy heart with all diligence; for out of it are the issues of life."*

In those days, the soldiers would wear a breastplate that would cover them from their chest down to their waist. If their armor had a crack in it, it would give the enemy an advantage. I don't want any cracks in my armor. I don't want to give the enemy an advantage in my life.

Let me say this: if there is any unconfessed sin in your life, then you are living with cracks and gaps in your armor. You are a walking target of opportunity for Satan!

## The Gospel of Peace

The next thing he mentions is our feet. Verse 15 says, *"And your feet shod with the preparation of the gospel of peace;"* What is the *"preparation of the gospel of peace"*?

Some say that having your feet shod with the *"preparation of the gospel of peace"* refers to our readiness and preparedness to walk in the *"gospel of peace."* The gospel of Christ brings peace so we should be prepared to take that gospel of peace to others, too.

Having the feet shod or protected is very important for a soldier in combat. If a soldier's feet were wounded, then he could no longer stand to fight or defend himself. A soldier was always to keep his feet shod so he could always be ready to move if needed.

Likewise, we must always be ready to share this gospel of peace with those we come in contact with because, not only is the gospel of peace important for us, it is VITALLY important for the world! The world is looking for peace, but they will never find true peace until they find the Prince of Peace!

## The Shield of Faith

The next thing Paul mentions is our shield. He says, *"Above all, taking the shield of faith, wherewith ye shall be able to quench all the fiery darts of the wicked"* (Eph. 6:16).

Notice it doesn't say that the shield of faith will only help you quench SOME of the fiery darts of the wicked.

"Well, Preacher, there is no way a teenager today can stay pure in this day. There's just too much temptation. It's not possible!" That is not what the Bible says. The Bible says that when Satan shoots the fiery dart of impurity at that teenager, if he is holding up the shield of faith, he can quench that fiery dart.

The word *"quench"* means "to extinguish." When you are daily saturating yourself with the Word of God, it has a cleansing affect that will extinguish those fiery temptations that will come your way.

The point is not only does it quench SOME of the fiery darts, it will quench ALL of them!

"But it is just too difficult to live for God today." Yes it is, without the shield of faith.

We better get back to teaching our young people that there is a fixed standard of right and wrong and it is called the Word of God. It is not what the school says or what the Supreme Court says. It is what God says that matters.

We live in a day where no one wants to believe in absolutes. But the Bible is FULL of absolutes. God did not give Moses the Ten Suggestions. He gave him the Ten Commandments. God's Word has some absolutes and our children need to hear those absolutes.

When we say to our children, "NO, you can't do that" and they ask why, we can't just say, "Because you shouldn't." That is not enough. We need to show them from the Bible why it is wrong. The problem is that parents many times don't even know what the Bible says themselves. We need to KNOW what the Bible says so we can SHOW them what the Bible says.

## The Helmet of Salvation

Next, Paul says we need *"the helmet of salvation."* A helmet protects the head. Imagine if a football player tried to play football without a helmet. He wouldn't make it more than a play or two!

The helmet of salvation protects our head; it helps to keep our minds right. With so much evil that is accessible today via the internet, it is so easy for Satan to get control of our minds. It is amazing how twisted some people's minds have become.

I remember watching a television special on a show called *Dateline*. They got undercover police officers to log on to internet chat rooms pretending to be under-age teenagers. Before long they would see child predators begin talking to them and would eventually set up a meeting with them thinking they were going to meet with that under-age child.

The television producers set up hidden cameras at a specified house where the predators were to come. It almost made my skin crawl to watch grown men drive long distances to meet up with young teenagers.

What made these men want to do such a thing? Somewhere along the way, they allowed Satan to control their thinking. Their minds had been filled with so much garbage that Satan had a hold of them. A person who is devil-controlled is not in his right mind.

Remember the maniac of Gadara in Mark 5? He was possessed by a devil and was going crazy. But when

Jesus saved him and took control, something happened.

> *And they come to Jesus, and see him that was possessed with the devil, and had the legion, sitting, and clothed, and in his right mind: and they were afraid. (Mark 5:15)*

That is why we must put on this armor every day. Paul challenges us in Romans 12 to do just that.

> *I beseech you therefore, brethren, by the mercies of God, that ye present your bodies a living sacrifice, holy, acceptable unto God, which is your reasonable service. And be not conformed to this world: but be ye transformed by the renewing of your mind, that ye may prove what is that good, and acceptable, and perfect, will of God. (Rom. 12:1-2)*

## The Sword of the Spirit

The next part of the armor Paul says we need is in verse 17. He says we need *"the sword of the Spirit, which is the word of God:"*

Since Jesus is our example, we might want to examine how He defeated Satan when He was tempted. You might say, "It was easy for Jesus; He was able to defeat Satan because He was God."

Yes, it is true that Jesus is God, but Jesus did not defeat Satan as God, He did it as man using the sword of the Spirit.

The Bible says in Hebrews chapter 4 that Jesus was tempted in all points like we are, *"yet without sin."* The reason He only used the Word of God was because He knew that was all we would have to defeat Satan with. Therefore, He wanted to show us that the Word of God is all we would really need.

He was tempted the same way you are tempted, and He won the battle the same way you can win the battle, with *"the sword of the Spirit which is the Word of God."*

Luke 4:1 tells us that Jesus was *"full of the Holy Ghost."* He was *"full."* If you are filled with something, there is no room for anything else. When you are filled with the Holy Spirit, then you cannot be filled with sin. If, on the other hand, you are filled with anger, lust, gossip or bitterness, you are not *"full of the Holy Ghost."*

In the world we live in, everywhere you look there is wickedness trying to get into our minds. How can we survive the attacks we face every day? We need to be *"full of the Holy Ghost."* We should respond the way Jesus did.

*And Jesus answered him, saying, It is written, That man shall not live by bread alone, but by every word of God. (Luke 4:4)*

*And Jesus answered and said unto him, Get thee behind me, Satan: for it is written, Thou shalt worship the Lord thy God, and him only shalt thou serve. (Luke 4:8)*

*And Jesus answering said unto him, It is said, Thou shalt not tempt the Lord thy God. (Luke 4:12)*

How did Jesus counter these temptations that came His way? He used the Sword of the Spirit by simply quoting scripture! We have one of the greatest weapons available to us, yet we never use it. The Word of God is powerful! "How powerful," you ask?

*For the word of God is quick, and powerful, and sharper than any twoedged sword, piercing even to the dividing asunder of soul and spirit, and of the joints and marrow, and is a discerner of the thoughts and intents of the heart. (Heb. 4:12)*

## Paul says, "Speak up!"

Finally, in verse 18, Paul says we should be *"Praying always with all prayer and supplication in the Spirit, and watching thereunto with all perseverance and supplication for all saints;"* None of the rest of the armor will help us very much if we do not pray. God wants us to speak up. He wants us to talk to Him.

Most of our prayers are to make the comfort level of our lifestyle go up. But that is not praying in the Spirit. So what does it mean to pray in the Spirit? It means to let the Holy Spirit energize your prayers and direct your prayers. It means praying that God's will might be done, instead of your will being done.

Notice that last phrase again in verse 18: *"with all perseverance and supplication for all saints;"* Paul closed the entire chapter speaking on the armor of God and how to defeat Satan by saying, *"Pray for each other."* Why is this important? Because not only are you facing Satan's attacks every day, but so is everyone else! We need to pray for each other.

Husbands need to pray for their wives and wives need to pray for their husbands. Parents need to pray for their children and children need to be praying for their parents. The Pastor needs to pray for the congregation and the congregation needs to be praying for their pastor.

The last verse Paul writes in this chapter is verse 24: *"Grace be with all them that love our Lord Jesus Christ in sincerity. Amen."* The word *"Grace"* means "a divine influence upon the heart." What is Paul saying?

There may be some Christian who gets into a deep struggle against temptation this week and, just when they are about to give in, some dear saint of God, not knowing what they are facing, begins praying for them. All of the sudden, the power of God gives them strength to resist that temptation and come out victoriously!

Since we all face temptations and attacks against our minds, we need to pray for one another. Praying for one another could be a matter of life or death for someone spiritually! We must not let Satan have control of our minds.

# CHAPTER 6

# 7 Steps To Winning the Battle

Satan wants to corrupt our minds and our children's minds. Because of that, we must not be ignorant of Satan's tactics. That is what this book is all about—making you aware of Satan's DEVICES but also making you aware of God's DEFENSES.

You might say, "But I have already fallen to one of Satan's attacks. What now?" Understand that no one is above Satan's attacks. We all fall from time to time. But as I wrote in my book, *RESTORATION: There's Life After The Locust,* failure doesn't have to be final! It is possible to be restored again once you have fallen.

In fact, here's a great way to respond after you fall. Just say to yourself, "I may have fallen, but I am going to start over and try to do it right this time." In other words, let every failure be an opportunity for you to get up and go for God again!

A successful football player goes out on the field expecting to be knocked down. But he also goes on the field knowing that if he is knocked down, he will get back up and go for the goal again. Could you imagine seeing a player run to the sideline after he got knocked down and saying to his coach, "Coach, I quit. Every time I run a play, somebody over there keeps knocking me down! I'm beginning to think they don't like me." That would be absurd. A successful football player is one who keeps getting up and going again **after** he gets knocked down.

That is also the definition of a successful Christian. A successful Christian is not one who never gets knocked down. It is not some SUPER-SAINT. It is simply a person who gets back up and picks up where they left off.

In this book, we have seen that the Bible has a lot to say about the mind and about our thoughts. Sometimes the mind is referred to as the heart.

*Keep thy heart with all diligence; for out of it are the issues of life. (Prov. 4:23)*

*For as he thinketh in his heart, so is he... (Prov. 23:7)*

We have also seen that it is up to us to do everything we can to guard our HEARTS and protect our HOMES from the attacks of Satan. Thankfully, we have the power of the Word of God from which we can draw strength to defend ourselves and control our thought lives.

In Psalm 119, the psalmist gives us the secret to winning the battle over the control of our minds. The secret is 8 specific steps we can take to ensure we keep a clean mind.

## Step #1: Get Clean

The psalmist begins in verse 9 by saying, *"Wherewithal shall a young man cleanse his way? by taking heed thereto according to thy word."*

The Bible says that you can be totally clean. The word *"way"* is a Hebrew word that means "in a rut, or a groove or a filthy way." How does a person get out of a rut or pattern of wicked thoughts? The first step toward victory is getting clean. Before you can STAY clean, you've got to GET clean, and the first step in

GETTING clean is COMING clean—admitting you have sin in your life.

One of the biggest struggles people face is the willingness to admit they've sinned. It is never their fault; it is someone else's fault that they sinned. We are very good at playing the "Blame Game." And we should be; we've been playing it since Adam started it in the Garden of Eden.

> *And the LORD God called unto Adam, and said unto him, Where art thou? And he said, I heard thy voice in the garden, and I was afraid, because I was naked; and I hid myself. And he said, Who told thee that thou wast naked? Hast thou eaten of the tree, whereof I commanded thee that thou shouldest not eat? And the man said,* **The woman whom thou gavest to be with me,** *she gave me of the tree, and I did eat. (Gen. 3:9-12)*

I can imagine how Adam must have tried to weasel his way out of being accountable for his sin.

When God came by, the day after Adam and Eve fell into sin, I can imagine Adam saying, "Oh, hello God. Yes, I know things don't look too good right now but you have to understand it's not MY fault! I wouldn't have fallen into sin on my own. I mean, there I was just minding my own business. When out of the blue Eve comes up to me with a piece of fruit and she tempts me. Can you believe that? Eve, the woman You created from my side, tempted me."

That might sound funny to you, but there are people today who use excuses that are just as crazy. Sadly, we live in a day where few people accept responsibility for their actions. The Bible says, *"If we say that we have no sin, we deceive ourselves, and the truth is not in us"* (1 John 1:8). David said, *"I will declare mine iniquity; I will be sorry for my sin"* (Ps. 38:18).

If you have a secret addiction, you need to realize that it is not a secret. God knows all about it! David realized his sin was not hidden when he prayed, *"For I acknowledge my transgressions: and my sin is ever before me. Against thee, thee only, have I sinned, and done this evil in thy sight"* (Ps. 51:3-4). David realized that God saw it all! Nothing was hid from Him.

You might say, "My sin isn't hurting anyone." But that is not true. First of all it is hurting YOU! Sin separates us from God and brings us under His judgment. I promise you, His judgment will hurt you. Secondly, your sin is hurting those around you. It hurts your spouse. It hurts your children. It affects your relationships. But most of all, it hurts GOD! It breaks His heart when we sin and our fellowship with Him is broken.

So how do we get clean? We are cleansed through obeying the Word of God. Jesus said in John 15:3, *"Now ye are clean through the word which I have spoken unto you."*

Can you imagine Jesus coming into your mind and making it totally clean? The good news is THAT CAN HAPPEN! 1 John 1:9 says, *"If we confess our sins, he is faithful and just to forgive us our sins, and to cleanse us from all unrighteousness."* Jesus not only forgives us; He also cleanses us when we repent of our sin.

So, the first step toward victory is confessing any sin you have in your life and allowing Jesus Christ to forgive you and cleanse you.

## Step #2: Be Determined

The next step he gives us is in verse 10. He says, *"With my whole heart have I sought thee: O let me not wander from thy commandments."*

First, there is a purification that says we need to GET clean, and then there is a determination that says we need to STAY clean.

The biggest problem is not that we do not want to confess our sin. The biggest problem is that we go right back to our sin after we've confessed it because we have failed to seek God with our whole heart.

The Psalmist said, *"With my* **whole heart** *have I sought thee:"* Sin cannot have a place in your heart if it is given completely to God.

Can you say that you are consumed with God and His Word? The reason many are stuck in a rut or pattern of sin is because they only make half-hearted spiritual decisions. The only way to have true victory is to make a whole-hearted decision to stay clean.

> *But if from thence thou shalt seek the LORD thy God, thou shalt find him, if thou seek him with all thy heart and with all thy soul. (Deut. 4:29)*

You will never win the battle over your mind if you only fight half-heartedly. Satan does not fight half-heartedly. Peter says that *"the devil, as a roaring lion, walketh about, seeking whom he may devour:"* (1 Pet. 5:8). A lion does not play around. A lion will not stop until it devours its prey. If you try to fight a lion half-heartedly you will lose, and you will lose if you fight Satan half-heartedly, too!

You cannot get married half-heartedly. Imagine it is your wedding day. Everyone is there and you are standing before the preacher. He looks at you and says, "Do you take her to be your lawfully wedded wife; to have and to hold from this day forward; in sickness and in health, so long as you both shall live?" What if you answered, "Maybe"? That wedding would soon turn into a funeral! No. You must make a whole-hearted decision to marry her.

You cannot go to Heaven half-heartedly. Salvation is a free gift from God to everyone who will repent and put their faith and trust in Him as their Lord and Savior. But you cannot receive Him as your Savior half-heartedly. It is either all or nothing! Likewise, when it comes to fighting Satan, we must do so with our whole heart.

You are not fighting Satan whole-heartedly when you come to church only once or twice a month, read your Bible when you remember to bring it to church, or pray only when something goes wrong.

Have you ever wondered why you never can seem to get the victory in your life? It is because you cannot get the victory when you're fighting the battle half-heartedly. If you do not determine to live for God, you will never experience true victory.

James says it this way: *"Submit yourselves therefore to God. Resist the devil, and he will flee from you"* (James 4:7). Here's the problem: you cannot resist the Devil if you haven't fully submitted to God.

Next, James says, *"Draw nigh to God, and he will draw nigh to you. Cleanse your hands, ye sinners; and purify your hearts, ye double minded"* (v.8). This verse contains three things WE are commanded to do: Draw nigh to God, cleanse our hands, and purify our hearts. This is part of us submitting ourselves to God.

Some people think that spirituality just happens. They think you just wake up one morning and...BOOM! You're spiritual! It doesn't happen that way. Spirituality begins with a determination we must have.

James says, *"Cleanse your hands,"* but here's the other problem. We may be cleansing our hands, but we are not purifying our hearts. A murderer could kill someone, then go home, take a shower, and change clothes. Is he still a murderer? After all, he did clean his hands. Yes, he cleaned his hands, but he didn't cleanse his heart. He still has murder in his heart.

Cleaning up the outside without cleaning up the inside will cause us to become double-minded. And when we become double-minded, then we become unstable. James 1:8 says, *"A double minded man is unstable in all his ways."*

Parents, when your children are small you might get away with being unstable in your Christian life. You can be unfaithful to church and they will think nothing of it. But the older they get, they will learn right away that mom and dad are hypocrites because they live one way at church and another way at home. And the best way to insure your children never want anything to do with God is to let them see a mom and dad who are double-minded.

The Bible says in Daniel chapter 1 that he did not defile himself by eating the king's meat. How did he do that? The Bible says that Daniel *"purposed in his heart"* (Daniel 1:8).

That's where it starts! Someone said, "God only DOES business with those who MEAN business!" If you are going to stay clean once you get clean, it will take determination.

## Step #3: Memorize Scripture

Next, the Psalmist says in verse 11, *"Thy word have I hid in mine heart, that I might not sin against thee."* In order to ensure we stay clean, we need to replace the sinful thoughts with the Word of God.

I remember hearing the story of a man who had gotten saved but he couldn't quit smoking. He went to his pastor for some advice. The pastor told him to put a New Testament in his shirt pocket where he previously kept his cigarettes. Every time he was tempted to get a cigarette, he would take out his New Testament instead and read it.

Eventually, the habit he developed of reading the Bible when he was tempted gave him victory over the habit of smoking.

The same thing applies to your thought life. If you are plagued with sinful thoughts that are difficult to stop, try this. Hide God's Word in your heart. It works!

"But how do I get it into my heart," you ask? You hide God's Word in your heart by memorizing it. "What? Memorize Scripture? You don't understand, I do not have a very good memory." Well, that is not necessarily true. You probably have a better memory than you think. You have just put it to use in other areas.

For example, some could not accurately name the Books of the Bible in order, but they can tell you the stats of their favorite players in every sport they watch. While memorizing sports stats is not bad, it will not give you victory over your thought life like memorizing Scripture can.

Why is memorizing Scripture so important? Because the Bible is the mind of God. Think about it. When you memorize Scripture, you are putting the mind of God into your mind. Now that is what I call being protected!

The Bible says, *"Let this mind be in you, which was also in Christ Jesus"* (Phil. 2:5). The more we put God's Word into our hearts through memorization, the more we will have the mind of Christ and will begin thinking like He thinks.

> *Finally, brethren, whatsoever things are true, whatsoever things are honest, whatsoever things are just, whatsoever things are pure, whatsoever things are lovely, whatsoever things are of good report; if there be any virtue, and if there be any praise, think on these things. Those things, which ye have both learned, and received, and heard, and seen in me, do: and the God of peace shall be with you. (Phil. 4:8-9)*

## Step #4: Remain Teachable

Next, He says in verse 12, *"Blessed art thou, O LORD: teach me thy statutes."* This step is very important because at this point you have gotten clean, determined to stay clean, and have begun to memorize Scripture. Now, you are open to the potential of becoming prideful; thinking you have arrived because you are working so hard at it.

In order for you to guard your heart and mind from allowing pride to build up, you will need to have a teachable spirit.

All through the Book of Proverbs we are warned about the dangers of not listening to wise advice.

*The way of a fool is right in his own eyes: but he that hearkeneth unto counsel is wise. (Prov. 12:15)*

*He that walketh with wise men shall be wise: but a companion of fools shall be destroyed. (Prov. 13:20)*

*A fool despiseth his father's instruction: but he that regardeth reproof is prudent. (Prov. 15:5)*

*He that refuseth instruction despiseth his own soul: but he that heareth reproof getteth understanding. (Prov 15:32)*

You can do anything with a person who accepts instruction and is teachable. On the other hand, you can do nothing with a person who thinks they already know it all! Sadly, there are many spiritual "know-it-alls" and that is why they are losing the battle with their minds.

Understand that there is much you can still learn. Go to church asking God to teach you something from the sermon. As you daily read your Bible, ask God to make it real to you. Many times the problem is that the Word of God is not real to us. We read it like a TEXTBOOK and not like a LOVE LETTER.

Here's a great prayer to pray, *"Open thou mine eyes, that I may behold wondrous things out of thy law"* (Ps. 119:18).

If you want victory over your mind, you must remain teachable.

## Step #5: Be Vocal

You've heard the expression "Children are to be seen and not heard." Well, that is definitely not true about a child of God. The psalmist says in verse 13, *"With my lips have I declared all the judgments of thy mouth."*

If you are going to win the battle over your mind, another step toward doing so is by keeping God's Word on your lips. CONfession and PROfession are linked together. Once you **confess** to God, you begin to **profess** with your lips.

It concerns me when I see people at church who never open their mouths and sing with everyone else. They have a sullen look on their faces and the appearance of no joy in their hearts. The Bible says that if you have been saved, God puts a new song in your heart. So if you are not singing, there must be a reason.

David spoke of the song that God puts into the heart of a believer, when he wrote:

> *"He brought me up also out of an horrible pit, out of the miry clay, and set my feet upon a rock, and established my goings. And he hath put a new song in my mouth, even praise unto our God: many shall see*

*it, and fear, and shall trust in the LORD"* (Ps. 40:2-3).

Too many times what comes out of our mouth is not pleasing to God. Paul said we are to *"put off concerning the former conversation the old man, which is corrupt according to the deceitful lusts"* (Eph. 4:22). Our conversation should honor the Lord.

## Step #6: Learn What Is Really Important

The next verse says, *"I have rejoiced in the way of thy testimonies, as much as in all riches"* (v.14). The psalmist said, "While most people only rejoice in getting the riches of this world, I've learned to rejoice in what is really important, the way of God's testimonies."

In other words, he found that true happiness comes from obeying God's Word.

The average Christian today has forgotten what is really important. They are searching for happiness in the things of this world and they are coming up empty! But Jesus told us how to find happiness.

He said in (John 13:17), *"If ye know these things, happy are ye if ye do them."* Happiness comes from obeying God's Word.

## Step #7: Meditate On God's Word

Verses 15-16 says, *"I will meditate in thy precepts, and have respect unto thy ways. I will delight myself in thy statutes: I will not forget thy word."* That's how you keep your mind clean and pure; don't forget His Word!

Later in this same chapter, he says, *"O how love I thy law! it is my meditation all the day"* (Ps. 119:97). It will be very difficult for you to dwell on sinful thoughts if your meditation is the Word of God *"all the day"* because God's Word has a cleansing affect.

### *Brainwashed*

The story is told of a missionary who was imprisoned by the Japanese in China. At this concentration camp, the penalty for owning even a portion of the Scriptures was death; however, a small Gospel of John was smuggled to her in a winter coat.

At night when she went to bed, she pulled the covers over her head and, with her flashlight in hand, read a verse and then put herself to sleep memorizing that verse.

In this way, over a period of time, she memorized the entire Gospel of John.

When she went to wash her hands she would take one page at a time, dissolve it with soap and water, and flush it down the drain. "And that is the way," she said, "that *John* and I parted company."

This little missionary was interviewed by a *Time* reporter just before the prisoners were released and he happened to be standing by the gates when the prisoners came out. Most of them shuffled along, eyes on the ground, looking almost like emotionless zombies. Then out came the missionary, as bright as a button. One of the reporters was heard to ask, "I wonder if they managed to brainwash her?" The *Time* reporter overheard the remark and answered, "God washed her brain."

That, my friend, is the secret to winning the battle over your mind. You must let God, through His Word, wash your brain and your mind on a daily basis.

*And be not conformed to this world: but be ye transformed by the renewing of your mind, that ye may prove what is that good, and acceptable, and perfect, will of God. (Rom. 12:2)*

# CHAPTER 7

# What Does God Think About?

Has it ever occurred to you that nothing has ever occurred to God? I mean, really. Think about it. There has never been a time when God has said to Himself, "Hmm. I didn't know that." God knows everything. The Bible says that nothing is hid from Him. God is both omniscient and omnipresent.

Therefore, a natural question comes to mind: if God is everywhere, sees everything, and knows everything, then what does *He* think about? Since He cannot sin, He doesn't have to think about how to get out of the trouble He has gotten Himself into like we do.

As a child, I remember having to rake leaves as one of my chores. One day I found an old aerosol paint can that still had a little paint left in it. For some unknown reason, I lit a match and thought I would put it out by spraying it with the aerosol can. BIG MISTAKE!

As soon as the paint hit the flame it turned that can into a torch! I thought the can was going to explode so I dropped it and the match and ran away. What I didn't realize was that when I dropped the match into the pile of leaves, it had not gone out.

A few minutes later, I turned around to find the entire pile of leaves had caught fire and as a result had caught the nearby grass on fire! I ran to the house and got the water hose, hoping to quickly put it out before my dad would notice the inferno outside.

I turned the water on and ran toward the fire with the hose. Now I had another problem. The hose would not reach! And of course, at the worst possible time, my dad came out the door. His eyes got as big as softballs and he yelled out, "Mark!" I turned around, trying to act as if nothing was wrong and said, "Why, hello father. How are you, today?"

"How did that fire start?" he asked.

Trying not to look suspicious I said, "What fire?" It didn't work; he knew better. He helped me get buckets to fill with water and we were eventually able to put the fire out.

In that split second when I had been caught by my dad, I was trying to figure out a way to get myself out of the mess I was in. God, however, is not like that. He never gets into trouble so He never has to waste His mental energy trying to get Himself out.

Then what exactly DOES He think about? Well, according to the Bible, He thinks about us! Notice what the following verses say about the thoughts of God.

## His Thoughts of Us Are PURPOSEFUL

*The counsel of the LORD standeth for ever, the* **thoughts** *of his heart to all generations. (Ps. 33:11)*

The word *"thoughts"* in this verse means "a plan or purpose." God does not have random thoughts that have no meaning or purpose to them. God's thoughts of us are in relation to His plan and our purpose in His plan. It also says that His plan and purpose is *"to all generations."*

Think about the very first generation that began way back in the Garden of Eden. How special it must have been to be a part of that generation. Everything was new and exciting. Every day must have been a new adventure.

Also think about the generation that was living at the time Christ was born and had the privilege of witnessing His ministry on Earth. They got to see firsthand the miracles we only read about in the Bible. What an honor it must have been to be a part of that generation and personally experience the resurrection of Christ.

And let's not forget our generation. Sure there is much that is wrong with our generation, but this is still one of the greatest times to be alive. We get to enjoy some of the greatest technological advances known to man and just may be alive to witness the rapture as well!

Every generation has had its blessings as well as its burdens. But He has always had a plan and a purpose for every generation.

## His Thoughts of Us Are PLENTIFUL

*Many, O LORD my God, are thy wonderful works which thou hast done, and thy **thoughts** which are to us-ward: they cannot be reckoned up in order unto* *thee: if I would declare and speak of them, they are more than can be numbered. (Ps. 40:5)*

There is no way we could count up the sum total of thoughts God has had of us, and STILL has. Their number would exceed our human mathematical possibilities.

"What all could He possibly be thinking of me," you ask? His thoughts are from all eternity. He has no doubt thought of the time He lovingly scooped up dirt and formed the very first man. He has thought of the time when he put Adam to sleep and took one of his ribs to create him a wife.

After that, He probably thought about man's fall in the Garden which brought sin, suffering, hurt and heartache into our lives and ruined this beautiful oasis God created called earth.

Then His thoughts turned toward His plan to redeem us back to Himself. He has thought of our pardon from sin and how that through the blood of Jesus Christ, God's only Son, we have been restored to Him again.

But His thoughts of us do not end there. He no doubt thinks of a time in the near future when He will send that same Son, Jesus, back to catch us away where we will live with Him forever and ever! It is easy to see how that His thoughts toward us *"are more than can be numbered."*

## His Thoughts of Us Are PEACEFUL

*For I know the thoughts that I think toward you, saith the LORD, thoughts of peace, and not of evil, to give you an expected end. (Jer. 29:11)*

It is sad that some people view God as an ogre up in Heaven just waiting for us to mess up so He can strike us with a bolt of lightning. But He is not like that at all! His thoughts toward us are of peace, not evil.

True, we do not always understand the circumstances He allows to come into our lives. But we must remember that His thoughts are so much higher than ours and *"His ways,"* the Bible says, are *"past finding out"* (Rom. 11:33).

*For my thoughts are not your thoughts, neither are your ways my ways, saith the LORD. For as the heavens are higher than the earth, so are my ways higher than your ways, and my thoughts than your thoughts. (Isa. 55:8-9)*

It would short-circuit your brain if you tried to think thoughts as high as God's thoughts. Everything we see, hear and touch in creation was a manifested thought of

God; it must have existed in his mind before it took shape, color or substance. It is amazing to think that the sea, sky, flowers and trees were thoughts of God. All the things we enjoy in creation are there because they were first in the mind of God.

Even more amazing is the fact that as a child of God, we can daily receive the thoughts of God into our souls from His Word! If you ever want to know what God thinks, you are as close to His thoughts as the nearest Bible!

## His Thoughts of Us Are PRECIOUS

*How precious also are thy thoughts unto me, O God! how great is the sum of them! (Ps. 139:17)*

The word *"precious"* refers to something that is prized because it is valuable. What a blessing to think that God thinks of us because we are valuable to Him. "How are we valuable to God," you ask? We are valuable to Him because He purchased us with the blood of His Son, Jesus. That was the greatest price that could have been paid.

It doesn't make any sense otherwise why God would think of us. The writer of Hebrews said, *"What is man, that thou art mindful of him"* (Heb. 2:6).

David said, *"But I am poor and needy; yet the Lord thinketh upon me: thou art my help and my deliverer"* (Ps. 40:17).

He thinks of us because He loves us. And He loves us so much that He sent Jesus to die as payment for our sin debt.

You can win the battle over your mind, but only through the power of the Word of God and the Holy Spirit. If you have never trusted in Jesus Christ as your Lord and Savior, you do not have the Holy Spirit living inside you to help you win the battle.

Call on Jesus today. Pray and tell Him that you realize that you are a sinner and that you do not deserve to go to Heaven. Tell Him that you believe He died, was buried, and rose again on the third day to pay for your sin. Put your faith and trust in Him, and Him alone, to forgive your sin and take you to Heaven when you die.

Because Jesus won the battle over sin, you can win the battle over your mind.

# ABOUT THE AUTHOR

Mark Agan is the youngest son of Champ & Dianne Agan and a third-generation pastor.

After High School, he attended Baptist University of America and then went on to Tabernacle Baptist Bible College in Greenville, South Carolina where Dr. Harold Sightler was the pastor.

In 1989, he married his wife, Beth. They have two sons: Tyler and Anthony.

In 2000, after having pastored his first church, the Lord led his family to plant an Independent Baptist church in Switzerland, Florida where the Lord blessed and they saw many saved. It was there that he was able to finish his education and earn a Doctorate of Theology (Th.D) degree from Slidell Baptist Seminary.

In 2008, they moved to Siler City, North Carolina, and he became the pastor of Community Baptist Church. Under his leadership, Community Baptist Church has seen steady growth and has become one of the most exciting churches in central North Carolina.

Made in the USA
Lexington, KY
01 August 2013